Morning Moon

written by Patricia M. Ware

Tate Publishing & *Enterprises*

This title is also available as a Tate Out Loud product.
Visit www.tatepublishing.com for more information.

Published by Tate Publishing & Enterprises, LLC
127 E. Trade Center Terrace | Mustang, Oklahoma 73064 USA
1.888.361.9473 | www.tatepublishing.com

Tate Publishing is committed to excellence in the publishing industry. The company reflects the philosophy established by the founders, based on Psalm 68:11,
"The Lord gave the word and great was the company of those who published it."

Cover and interior design by Elizabeth M. Hawkins
Illustrations by Kathy Hoyt

Published in the United States of America

ISBN: 978-1-61663-917-4
Juvenile Nonfiction / Poetry / General
10.07.16

For Olivia, our Little Gal, who inspired the story.

OLIVIA

How strange,
in the middle of morning,
To see the moon
Peeping through my window.
It was nearly noon!

"Good morning, Moon,"
I said to him.
"Have you lost your way?
Did you miss the path to night
And stumble in to day?"

"Or were you told about the day
With sunshine, trees and flowers?
Did you want to see it all
So abandoned nighttime hours?"

"Are you lonely up there, Moon,
Without the stars about you?
Will they miss you, Moon,
And weep to be without you?"

"You've always brightened up the night.
Tonight, will you be there,
Or will I have to tell the stars
You've wandered off somewhere?"

"If I could stretch my hand up there
And hold you really tight,
Would you come along
And let me lead you back to night?"

"Or do you want to stay a while
To frolic with the sun,
Moonbeams chasing sunbeams,
Until the day is done?"

"I'm going out to play now, Moon.
I won't be long, all right?
I hope you're in the same old place
When I go to bed tonight."

listen|imagine|view|experience

AUDIO BOOK DOWNLOAD INCLUDED WITH THIS BOOK!

In your hands you hold a complete digital entertainment package. In addition to the paper version, you receive a free download of the audio version of this book. Simply use the code listed below when visiting our website. Once downloaded to your computer, you can listen to the book through your computer's speakers, burn it to an audio CD or save the file to your portable music device (such as Apple's popular iPod) and listen on the go!

How to get your free audio book digital download:

1. Visit www.tatepublishing.com and click on the e|LIVE logo on the home page.
2. Enter the following coupon code:
   4731-273b-fbc7-b2e0-66ab-0baa-23f7-d4dc
3. Download the audio book from your e|LIVE digital locker and begin enjoying your new digital entertainment package today!